Copyright © AskTheValuer 2023

All rights reserved. No part of this book may be reproduced or used in any form or by any means electronic or mechanical, including photocopying, recording, and/or by an information storage or retrieval system, whatsoever without prior written permission from the author.

Second Edition 2023

First published 2016

Disclaimer

This book aims to provide both general and specific information about Melbourne in particular, and Australia in general. While every reasonable effort has been made to ensure the accuracy and currency of the information herein, please note that details may change over time. Therefore, this information should not be relied upon as legal advice or a substitute for professional counsel. Additionally, individual circumstances can vary, and there may be legal requirements or other factors not covered in this book. No warranty or representation regarding the accuracy, completeness, or reliability of the information is made, and no liability is assumed for any errors or omissions in the book's content. Readers are advised to seek legal or other professional advice as appropriate, especially regarding their specific situations, before acting on any information in this book. The ideas or tips presented may not be suitable for everyone and are not guaranteed to produce any specific result.

Contents

This Book Could Change Your Life   1
1. Is Moving to a New City in a New Country Right for You?   5
2. Why Melbourne?   10
3. Melbourne, City of Opportunities   16
4. Where to Live in Melbourne?   32
5. Money Matters   39
6. Medical Care in Melbourne   54
7. Overcoming the Fear of Moving to a New City   57
8. What's Next?   63

APPENDICES   68

Appendix A   69
Appendix B   71
Appendix C   76
Appendix D   79

This Book Could Change Your Life

W ritten by a migrant for potential migrants, 'A New Life in Melbourne, Australia' aims to inspire your aspirations for a new life in a city brimming with opportunities. Melbourne, where nearly 31% of its almost 5 million residents are migrants, presents a dynamic setting for those dreaming of a fresh start in a place rich with possibilities and cultural diversity.

Part Guidebook, Part Self-Improvement Book

This book is part guidebook, part self-improvement book filled with information and ideas for the adventurous, ambitious or discontented. It's an ideal read for those open to life beyond familiar grounds, unafraid of change, and eager to embrace new experiences. If you have been contemplating a new start in a different city, this book will encourage you to take that brave leap. It is divided into 10 sections:

1 – Is a New City in a New Country Right for You?
2 – Why Melbourne?
3 – Melbourne, City of Opportunities
4 – Where to Live in Melbourne?
5 – Money Matters
6 – Your Home Options in Melbourne
7 – Medical Care in Melbourne
8 – Overcoming the Fear of Change
9 – What's Next?
Appendices

Who Can Benefit from Reading this Book?

In particular, it was written for you if you are:

- A discontented professional, businessperson, or university graduate, seeking new job or business opportunities in Melbourne;

- Someone who has achieved financial independence and is looking for a lifestyle change;

- A parent eager to give your child a brighter future;

- A forward-looking student planning to apply for permanent residency after completing tertiary studies in Melbourne; or

- Someone unhappy with your country's lack of freedom and corrupted government.

But this book could also be life-changing for:

- An overseas student who has recently graduated from an Australian university, or an expatriate who enjoys the Australian lifestyle, culture, and country;

- A loved one joining their Australian partner; or

- Anyone seeking a better quality of life.

What can You Benefit by Reading this Book?

This book has the potential to positively impact your life in many ways. Some of the main benefits from this book are as follows:

Provides valuable information: This book is designed to offer practical information about living in Melbourne, including topics such as housing, healthcare, education, employment, and culture. This information can help you make informed decisions and feel more confident about your transition to a new city.

Offers tips for adapting: Moving to a new city can be a challenging experience, but this book can provide you with strategies for adapting and thriving in your new environment. It may offer insights into how to make new friends, find local resources, and navigate the city's customs and culture.

Inspires motivation and action: This book may inspire you to act and make the most of your new life in Melbourne. It may provide you with ideas for new activities, events, or hobbies to explore, or inspire you to pursue new goals and ambitions.

Encourages personal growth: Moving to a new city can be a transformative experience, and this book may inspire you to grow and develop in new ways. It may encourage you to step outside of your comfort zone, try new things, and embrace new experiences, which can help you develop new skills, expand your perspective, and grow as a person.

Builds community: This book may spur you to connect with other newcomers and to the broader community in Melbourne. It may provide you with opportunities to meet other migrants, attend cultural events, or volunteer in the community, which can help you build meaningful connections and feel a sense of belonging.

Provides a sense of re-assurance: Moving to a new city can be overwhelming, but this book may provide you with a sense of reassurance that you are not alone. It may help you realise that many others have faced similar challenges and that there are resources and support available to help you navigate your transition to Melbourne.

Offers a sense of excitement: Moving to a new city can be a thrilling experience, and this book may help you tap into that sense of excitement and adventure. It may inspire you to explore new neighbourhoods, try new foods, and immerse yourself in the culture of Melbourne, which can help you build a strong connection to your new home.

Chapter One

Is Moving to a New City in a New Country Right for You?

"I am so thankful that I live in such a peaceful environment, not to mention the opportunities I have enjoyed as a migrant to this Lucky Country."

Countless individuals worldwide are eager to migrate to a more favourable country, willing to go to great lengths for this opportunity.

Why Migrate?

It is now April 2023. It was about two months since my wife, two daughters and I returned from Country X after a 4-week holiday. Since the 2016 description in the First Edition of this book, Country X's situation has remained largely unchanged, except for a newly elected government inheriting a corrupt system that has been in place for more than half a century.

First Edition 2016

It is a bright Saturday morning in late summer here in this lovely pocket of Glen Waverley, a suburb some 19 kilometres from the Melbourne Central Business District. Looking out of my study window I see the lovely white flowers hanging from the deciduous tree in front of my home against the quiet distant backdrop of my neighbours' landscaped gardens, lovely orange brick homes, and the row of towering Cyprus trees along a paved roadway. I can hear fluttering leaves as white pigeons fly to and from the tree in front of my house.

I am so thankful that I live in such a peaceful environment, not to mention the opportunities I have enjoyed as a migrant to this Lucky Country. Yes, Melbourne, Australia has been my home for over 25 years.

It was only three months ago when I travelled with my wife and two daughters to the country where I was born and lived until just before my twentieth birthday. I shall not disclose the name of this country for fear of any reprisal for what I am about to describe here.

Country X used to be a beautiful place to live in. The population comprising several different ethnic groups and religions lived in peace and harmony. People from different ethnic groups and religions befriended one another. They lived next door to each other. The children played with one another. The adults had meals and drinks together. Parties and functions were multi-racial events. Families visited each other during all the major religious festivals. There was no discrimination amongst the ethnic groups and religions. People dressed as they pleased. The cost of living was low. People could earn a decent living. There was not much traffic on the roads. The government was fair to everyone.

Fast forward to February 2016. Country X is in a mess! The cost of living has gone sky high. Large segments of the population live from month to month on their wages, even with two jobs or both husband and wife working. There is blatant racial discrimination, not much amongst the men, women and children in the street, but institutionalised discrimination, short of apartheid, because of decades of ethnic-based government policies. As a result, the minority ethnic groups in their own country of birth are feeling threatened, bullied and unwanted. Not too many years ago, criticising the leader or the government has landed many opposition politicians, academics, student leaders and even a cartoonist into hot soup, including imprisonment. Despite billions of dollars spent on highways, airports, high rise buildings, shopping malls, flood mitigation projects, etc. the capital and largest city in Country X suffer from massive traffic jams, flash floods, poorly maintained buildings, smelly places, potholes everywhere and overall, a lack of coordination in most of its systems. I can go on and on with a litany of grouses experienced daily by most of the population in Country X, but I am sure you got the point.

Besides Country X there are many other countries in the world where living conditions are even worse, the rule of law is lacking, opportunities to earn a decent income are few, and personal freedom is limited. Millions and millions of people all over the world would literally die to migrate to a better country.

The reasons for migration can vary widely and are often complex, with multiple factors playing a role in an individual's decision to move to another country. These could include:

Economic reasons: People may migrate to seek better job opportunities and higher wages than what is available in their home country.

Political reasons: People may migrate to escape persecution, violence, or political instability in their home country.

Education: People may migrate to pursue higher education or specialised training that is not available in their home country for themselves or their children.

Family reunification: People may migrate to be reunited with family members who have already migrated.

Natural disasters or environmental reasons: People may migrate due to natural disasters, such as hurricanes or earthquakes, or environmental reasons, such as drought or famine.

Health reasons: People may migrate to access better healthcare services than what is available in their home country.

Adventure or personal growth: Some people may migrate to experience new cultures and languages, challenge themselves, or explore new opportunities.

Moving to a New City

Moving to a new city can be exciting, but it can also be challenging. Here are some common challenges people may face when moving to a new city:

Finding a new home: Finding a new home can be challenging, especially if you are not familiar with the city. You may need to spend a lot of time researching neighbourhoods, rental prices, and transportation options.

Making new friends: Moving to a new city means leaving behind your old social circle. You will need to make an effort to meet new people and make new friends. This can be especially challenging if you are introverted or have a busy schedule.

Adjusting to a new environment: Every city has its own unique culture, customs, and way of life. Adjusting to a new environment can be difficult, especially if you are moving to a city that is very different from where you grew up.

Finding a job: If you are moving to a new city without a job, finding employment can be a challenge. You will need to research the job market, update your resume, and network with potential employers.

Dealing with homesickness: It is natural to miss your old home and the people you left behind. Dealing with homesickness can be challenging, especially in the early days of your move.

Navigating transportation: If you are moving to a new city, you will need to learn how to get around. This can be challenging if you are not used to using public transportation or navigating new roads.

Adapting to new weather patterns: Depending on where you are moving, the weather may be very different from what you are used to. Adjusting to new weather patterns can be challenging, especially if you are not used to extreme heat or cold.

Chapter Two

Why Melbourne?

To be ranked as the World's Most Liveable City just once by the Economist Intelligence Unit (EIU) is a great honour for any city. But to win the title *eight times* in a 10-year period (six of which were in a row from 2011 to 2016) is almost unbelievable.

World's Most Liveable City

Created in 1946 with offices worldwide, the EIU is a research and analysis firm and subsidiary of The Economist Group, a London-based media company that publishes The Economist magazine, widely regarded as one of the world's most influential publications on economics, finance, politics, and current affairs. The Global Liveability Index, which ranks cities around the world based on various factors that contribute to their overall liveability is also one of the EIU's most well-known publications.

The EIU's research and analysis are used by a range of organisations, including businesses, governments, and non-profit organisations, to inform decision-making and strategic planning.

Beating All Other Major Cities in the World

To win the title of World's Most Liveable City, depending on which year, Melbourne had to beat an average of 150 other well-known cities worldwide including those in the USA, Europe and Asia. The EIU assesses the liveability of cities around the world based on 30 factors, 10 of which are:

Stability – Factors included: crime rates, civil unrest, and threat of terrorism.

Healthcare – Factors included: availability of quality healthcare services, availability of over-the-counter drugs, and general healthcare infrastructure.

Culture and environment – Factors included: climate, level of corruption, social or religious restrictions, and quality of cultural and sporting events.

Education – Factors included: availability of international schools, quality of public and private education systems, and access to lifelong learning opportunities.

Infrastructure – Factors included: public transportation, quality of road networks, availability of housing, and access to utilities and communication networks.

Environment – Factors included: air quality, water quality, and access to green spaces.

Leisure – Factors included: availability of restaurants, theatres, and other recreational activities.

Safety – Factors included: level of violent crime and the effectiveness of law enforcement.

Political and social environment – Factors included: government stability, level of corruption, and social freedoms.

Economic environment – Factors included: job opportunities, income levels, and ease of doing business.

Here are the rankings of Melbourne from 2011 to 2023 in the Economist Intelligence Unit's Global Liveability Index:

2023: Melbourne ranked *third*, behind Vienna, Austria and Copenhagen, Denmark.

2022: See Note below.

2021: Melbourne ranked *second*, behind Auckland, New Zealand.

2020: Melbourne was *not included* in the ranking due to the COVID-19 pandemic.

2019: Melbourne ranked *second*, behind Vienna, Austria.

2018: Melbourne ranked *second*, behind Vienna, Austria.

2017: Melbourne ranked *first*, ahead of Vienna, Austria, and Vancouver, Canada.

2016: Melbourne ranked *first*, ahead of Vienna, Austria, and Vancouver, Canada.

2015: Melbourne ranked *first*, ahead of Vienna, Austria, and Vancouver, Canada.

2014: Melbourne ranked *first*, ahead of Vienna, Austria, and Vancouver, Canada.

2013: Melbourne ranked first, ahead of Vienna, Austria, and Vancouver, Canada.

2012: Melbourne ranked *first*, ahead of Vienna, Austria, and Vancouver, Canada.

2011: Melbourne ranked *first*, ahead of Vienna, Austria, and Vancouver, Canada.

Note: According to the EIU, Melbourne and other Australian cities fell in ranking in 2022 due to the impact of harsh COVID-19 restrictions. Melbourne was the most lockdown city in the world

What I personally like about Melbourne

As a long-time migrant, I can confidently say that Melbourne is generally clean, safe and orderly. It has a good road network – driving in Melbourne is generally pleasant; and an efficient public transport system – but the locals complain when the train or bus is 5 minutes late!

You can go almost anywhere throughout Melbourne at any time of the day or night and not feel threatened for your safety or wallet. If you live in a city where taking a wrong turn could mean an encounter with an undesirable situation for your safety or wallet, then you will appreciate how safe Melbourne is.

One thing that stands out to me about Melbourne is its commitment to inclusivity and diversity. The city has a large and active multicultural community, with people from all over the world calling it home. This diversity is reflected in the city's many festivals and events, which highlights a range of cultures and traditions. It is also known for its vibrant arts scene, with numerous museums, galleries, theatres, and music venues.

In addition to its vibrant culture, Melbourne also boasts pleasant and temperate weather that is perfect for outdoor activities throughout the year. The city is known for its four distinct seasons (sometimes in one day!), each of which has its own unique charm.

In summer, temperatures are usually in the mid-20s to low-30s Celsius (mid-70s to low-90s Fahrenheit), perfect for outdoor events. In autumn, colourful foliage creates a picturesque background for outdoor activities.

Melbourne's winter is cool and crisp, with temperatures in low- to mid-teens Celsius (low-50s to mid-60s Fahrenheit). Enjoy indoor activities like art galleries and music performances. In spring, blooming flowers and warming temperatures bring the city back to life.

Last but not least, what I particularly enjoy about Melbourne is the abundance and diversity of food options available which reflects the city's multi-cultural composition.

Note: Melbourne is both the name of the city that serves as the state capital of Victoria and the name of the municipality that comprises the central business district (CBD) and some surrounding areas such as Docklands and Southbank.

Short History of Melbourne

Melbourne has a fascinating history that spans over 60,000 years, starting with the Indigenous Australians who have lived on this land for thousands of years. Melbourne's location made it an ideal spot for Indigenous Australians to gather, trade, and conduct ceremonies, and there are many significant cultural sites throughout the city.

The Wurundjeri people are the traditional owners of the land on which Melbourne was built, and their cultural heritage is still celebrated today. The city has several significant Indigenous cultural sites, including the Birrarung Marr Park, which features a range of public artworks and installations that reflect the Indigenous history of the area.

In the 19th century, Melbourne was founded by Europeans who were attracted to the city's location on the Yarra River, which provided easy access to the port. The city grew rapidly during the gold rush of the 1850s, which brought tens of thousands of people to Melbourne in search of fortune. This influx of people led to the development of new suburbs and the construction of many significant buildings, such as the Royal Exhibition Building and Parliament House.

Melbourne played a significant role in Australia's federation in 1901, as it hosted the first meeting of the Australian Parliament. The city continued to grow and develop throughout the 20th century, with major infrastructure projects like the construction of the West Gate Bridge and the Melbourne Underground Rail Loop.

Today, Melbourne is a thriving metropolis with a rich history that is reflected in its architecture, cultural institutions, and public spaces. Exploring Melbourne's history is a great way to understand how the city has developed into the dynamic and diverse place that it is today.

Chapter Three

Melbourne, City of Opportunities

M elbourne is one of the most vibrant and prosperous cities in Australia and Oceania, with a diverse economy and a range of job and business opportunities across various sectors.

Job Opportunities in Melbourne

Some of the key industries in Melbourne include:

Education and research: Melbourne is home to some of Australia's leading universities and research institutions, including the University of Melbourne and Monash University. These institutions offer a range of job opportunities in research, teaching, administration, and support roles.

Healthcare: Melbourne has a strong healthcare industry, with numerous hospitals, clinics, and medical research facilities. There is a high demand for healthcare professionals, including doctors, nurses, and allied health professionals.

Information technology and digital media: Melbourne has a growing technology sector, with numerous startups and established tech companies. Job opportunities include software developers, data analysts, and digital media professionals.

Professional services: Melbourne has a large professional services sector, including accounting, legal, and consulting firms. Job opportunities include lawyers, accountants, and management consultants.

Creative industries: Melbourne has a thriving arts and culture scene, with numerous galleries, theatres, and music venues. There are job opportunities in various creative industries, including graphic design, advertising, and media production.

Manufacturing and engineering: Melbourne has a strong manufacturing and engineering sector, with numerous factories and engineering firms. Job opportunities include engineers, production managers, and technicians.

What about for new migrants

For new migrants to Melbourne, the job market can be competitive, but there are still plenty of opportunities available across different industries. Here are some tips for new migrants looking for job opportunities in Melbourne:

Research the job market: Before you start applying for jobs, it is important to research the job market in Melbourne and understand which industries and sectors are hiring. You can use job search websites like Seek, Indeed, and LinkedIn to browse job listings and learn more about different companies and industries.

Build your network: Networking is an important part of finding job opportunities in Melbourne. Attend industry events, join professional associations, and connect with people on LinkedIn to build your network and learn about job openings.

Tailor your resume and cover letter: When applying for jobs, make sure your resume and cover letter are tailored to the specific job and company you are applying to. Highlight your relevant skills and experience and explain how they make you a good fit for the position.

Consider temporary or contract work: Temporary or contract work can be an effective way to gain experience and build your network in Melbourne. Consider working with a staffing agency or taking on short-term assignments to gain experience and get your foot in the door.

Learn new skills: Consider taking courses or workshops to learn new skills that are in demand in Melbourne. This can help you stand out to employers and increase your job prospects.

Where to find Job Opportunities?

There are numerous job opportunities in Melbourne for new migrants. If you're not choosy and need some money quickly, finding a job that pays between A$20 to A$25 an hour is not difficult. Melbourne businesses and companies offer full time, part time and casual jobs or you may hear the words permanent or temporary jobs.

There are several resources available for finding job opportunities in Melbourne. Here are some of the most popular options:

Online job search websites: There are several job search websites that list job opportunities in Melbourne, including Seek, Indeed, LinkedIn, Gumtree, CareerOne,

Adzuna and Jora. These websites allow you to search for jobs by industry, location, and other criteria.

Company websites: Many companies in Melbourne list job opportunities on their websites. If you have a specific company in mind that you would like to work for, check their website for job listings.

Recruitment agencies: Recruitment agencies can help match you with job opportunities that fit your skills and experience. Some of the top recruitment agencies in Melbourne include Hays, Adecco, Robert Walters, Michael Page, Chandler Macleod and Manpower.

Networking: Building your professional network can be a terrific way to learn about job opportunities that may not be listed online. Attend industry events, connect with people on LinkedIn, and join professional associations to build your network.

Job fairs: Job fairs are events where multiple employers gather to meet with job seekers and discuss job opportunities. These events can be a wonderful way to meet employers and learn about job openings in Melbourne.

Job Categories

To give you some idea of the areas you could consider, here is a list:

- Accounting & Book-keeping
- Administration & Office Support
- Call Centre & Customer Service
- Construction & Building Trades
- Engineering & Technical Services
- Financial Services
- Graphic & Web Design
- Hotel & Restaurant
- Human Resources & Recruitment
- Import & Export
- Insurance
- Legal
- Manufacturing
- Medical & Health Services
- Pet Services
- Real Estate & Property
- Retail & Consumer Products
- Sales

- Taxi or Courier Services

- Teaching & Tutoring

- Transport & Logistics

- Wholesaling

- **Latest! AI job opportunities are now becoming widespread.**

Qualifications

To work in Melbourne the most important qualification is being able to speak English fluently. If you are from a non-English speaking country or background, you must usually pass an English test and possibly also an occupational English examination.

Next, you should find out whether your trade or professional qualifications are recognised in Australia. While you may be well qualified in your own country, you may need to pass professional examinations or trade tests to satisfy Australian standards.

Although qualifications recognised by professional and trade bodies overseas are usually recognised in Australia, this is not always the case. Likewise, all academic qualifications should also be recognised.

To work in Melbourne as a licensed trades person you must have your qualifications assessed by Trades Recognition Australia (TRA). You may also need to obtain a license (or pass an examination) to work in some professions or trades. TRA assesses migrants' experience, qualifications and skills against comparable standards in Australia.

For migrant professionals such as accountants, lawyers or doctors the recognition of their professional qualifications is usually the responsibility of the relevant professional body that migrants are required to join to practise in Australia. Some professional bodies require those from overseas to pass examinations conducted or supervised by themselves or in some cases for foreign professionals to work under the supervision of a recognised professional Australian for a period (e.g., a year or two), or to undertake further training.

You can check the qualifications required for a particular job in the Australian Standard Classification of Occupations (ASCO) dictionary, available for reference at Australian High Commission offices and other Australian government offices overseas, or on the website of the Australian Bureau of Statistics.

The qualifications required for jobs in Melbourne can vary widely depending on the industry and specific job. Here are some general guidelines for some of the most popular industries in Melbourne:

Education and research: Jobs in education and research typically require a university degree, such as a Bachelor's, Master's, or PhD degree, depending on the level of the job. Some jobs, such as teaching or research assistant positions, may require only a bachelor's degree.

Healthcare: Jobs in healthcare typically require a university degree, such as a bachelor's or master's degree in nursing, medicine, or allied health fields. Some jobs, such as medical assistants or home health aides, may require only a diploma or certificate from a vocational school.

Information technology and digital media: Jobs in IT and digital media typically require a degree in computer science, software engineering, or a related field. Some jobs, such as web developers or digital marketing specialists, may require only a diploma or certificate from a vocational school.

Professional services: Jobs in professional services, such as accounting, legal, or consulting, typically require a university degree, such as a bachelor's or master's degree in accounting, law, or business. Some jobs, such as administrative assistants or bookkeepers, may require only a diploma or certificate from a vocational school.

Creative industries: Jobs in creative industries, such as graphic design, advertising, or media production, typically require a university degree or diploma in a related field, such as graphic design, advertising, or film and media studies.

Manufacturing and engineering: Jobs in manufacturing and engineering typically require a university degree or diploma in engineering, manufacturing, or a related field. Some jobs, such as production line workers or machine operators, may require only a high school diploma or vocational training.

Business Opportunities in Melbourne

If finding a job is not your "cup of tea" because you do not want to work for someone else and you are willing to take risks, then a new life in Melbourne could mean starting a business. There are many business opportunities in Melbourne. Depending on your financial resources and circumstances you could consider buying an existing business or a franchise or start a business from scratch.

Melbourne is a hub for business and entrepreneurship, with a strong economy and a range of opportunities across different industries. Here are some examples of business opportunities in Melbourne:

Startups: Melbourne has a thriving startup scene, with numerous incubators, accelerators, and co-working spaces. There are opportunities to launch new businesses in industries such as technology, healthcare, and creative industries.

Franchising: Franchising can be a good option for entrepreneurs who want to start a business with an established brand and support system. Melbourne has a range of franchise opportunities in industries such as food and beverage, retail, and education.

Exporting: Melbourne has a strong trade and export industry, with opportunities to export products and services to other countries. The Victorian Government offers resources and support for businesses looking to expand into international markets.

Importing & Distribution: Melbourne offers a range of opportunities for importing and distribution businesses, particularly in food and beverage, consumer goods, automotive, industrial supplies and health and beauty products.

Manufacturing: Melbourne has a strong manufacturing industry, with opportunities to manufacture products in industries such as automotive, aerospace, and medical devices. The Victorian Government offers support and resources for businesses looking to invest in manufacturing.

Professional services: Melbourne has a large professional services sector, with opportunities for businesses in industries such as accounting, legal, and consulting. There is a high demand for professional services in Melbourne, particularly for businesses that offer specialised expertise or services.

Tips for Migrants

Here are some tips for migrants looking to start a business in Melbourne:

Research the market: Before starting a business in Melbourne, it is important to research the local market and understand the demand for your product or service. Talk to potential customers and partners, and research the competition to understand the market landscape.

Understand the legal and regulatory requirements: Starting a business in Australia requires registering your business with the Australian Securities and Investments Commission (ASIC) and complying with various legal and regulatory requirements. It is important to understand these requirements and seek out professional advice as needed.

Network and build relationships: Building a network of contacts and relationships can be a key factor in the success of your business. Attend industry events, join professional associations, and connect with people on LinkedIn to build your network and learn about potential partners and customers.

Consider seeking support and funding: There are numerous organisations in Melbourne that offer support and funding to new businesses, particularly those led by migrants. Some examples include the Victorian Small Business Commission and the Australian Government's Entrepreneurship Program.

Leverage your skills and experience: Your skills and experience as a migrant can be a unique asset in starting a business in Melbourne. Consider leveraging your language skills, cultural knowledge, and international contacts to build a business that serves the needs of other migrants or international markets.

Buying an Existing Business

Some of the advantages of buying an existing business include: (1) the business is already set up, no need to think of a name, design a logo and produce other marketing material; (2) no need to find premises and to fit out and furnish the place; (3) no need to start from the first customer, instead you continue serving existing customers; (4) using existing suppliers; and (5) a certain level of goodwill has been created.

The biggest risk in buying an existing business are the inflated claims by the seller relating to the sales, profitability and customers of the business. But there are ways to reduce this risk that are beyond the scope of this book.

Buying a Franchise

Advantages of buying a franchise include:

- You do not necessarily need to have business experience to run a franchise. Training is provided by the franchisor.

- No need to build a business from scratch as a franchise business will have systems in place for areas including marketing, management and work practices.

- You will benefit from an established name and ongoing support.

- As a franchise business owner, you have the independence of a small business owner but have the benefits of a big business network.

- Franchises have a higher rate of success than businesses starting from scratch.

Disadvantages of franchises include:

- Franchise agreements dictate how you run the business, so there may be little room for creativity.

- There are usually restrictions on your business location,

products you sell, selling prices and the suppliers you use.

Finding a Business or Franchise for Sale

In the age of the Internet, finding a business or franchise for sale has become effortless. You can find many Melbourne businesses for sale on business broker websites and franchises for sale online as well. It is best to consult a suitable local accountant before buying any business or franchise.

Here are several resources available for finding businesses for sale in Melbourne. Here are some options to consider:

Business brokers: Business brokers are professionals who specialise in buying and selling businesses. They have access to a wide range of businesses for sale and can help you find a business that fits your needs and budget. Some of the top business brokers in Melbourne include LINK Business, Business Sales Victoria, and GMO Business Sales.

Online business marketplaces: There are several online marketplaces that list businesses for sale in Melbourne, including businessesforsale.com.au, Bsale, and AnyBusiness. These websites allow you to search for businesses by industry, location, and other criteria.

Classified ads: Classified ads in newspapers or online can be a useful source of businesses for sale, particularly for small or local businesses. Check out websites like Gumtree or newspaper classified pages to find businesses for sale in Melbourne.

Networking: Networking with business owners and professionals in your industry can be a great way to learn about businesses for sale that may not be listed publicly. Attend industry events, connect with people on LinkedIn, and join professional associations to build your network.

Starting a Business from Scratch

If you do not think buying a business or a franchise is the best option, then you may consider starting a business from scratch. If you have skills in a trade such as carpentry, plumbing, electrical, tiling, glazing, locksmithing or gardening, you are in a good position for self-employment. There are many successful tradespersons who run an independent one-person business. However, most likely there will be trade qualifications that you would need to attain before you can charge for your services to the public.

Other popular businesses you could start including a food-related business, a specialist retail shop, an internet-related service provider, an in-demand service or a service related to visual communication.

Examples of a food related business are a cafe, restaurant, bar, food kiosk or takeaway. Your specialist retail shop could sell one of the following: mobile phones, footwear, clothing, health food or any products that you can see a gap in the Melbourne market. If you are an internet-related service provider you could be a website designer, content provider, SEO consultant or a virtual assistant. Some in-demand services you could offer could include tutoring groups of students at various levels; book-keeping and accounting services for other small businesses; and domestic and commercial cleaning. Services related to visual communications include photography, graphic design or illustration and video production.

Education for All Ages

Every parent desire a better future for their child. Chief among the ingredients for a better future is a good education. Every parent knows (or thinks) that a good education leads to a good job. Though generally true, the more important benefit from a good education is that it equips a person with the ability to research, analyse, plan, and think critically and constructively.

If you continue to live in the same place where you are now, what are the chances of your child (children) getting a place in the local university to study a course of his or her choice? Is university education expensive? Is it only for those who can afford or have connections? What is the standard of education in the place where you live? Are there many options on what and where to study?

Traditionally, people think of education as going to school, college, university or some institution where they end up with a degree or diploma of some sort. But education also includes learning a trade or vocation, preparing one to be, for example, an auto mechanic or a carpenter, confectioner, tailor, hairdresser, tiler, plumber, machinist, locksmith, fitness instructor or panel beater. Furthermore, education could also include a course in music, dance, theatre or visual arts.

In Melbourne, you will find numerous education opportunities that may not be readily available where you come from. Whether a university degree, a trade qualification or a certificate in visual communications, there is a place your child or even you can be educated.

In Melbourne and all of Australia, the traditional education pathway begins in primary school, then secondary school and continues through to a tertiary institution. Australian educational institutions, in particular tertiary level colleges of higher learning and universities, generally have a good international reputation. Melbourne's schools provide a high standard of teaching and produce good academic results. Quality and excellence can be found at every level of education.

In Melbourne, if the traditional education pathway to university that tends to be academic focus is not suitable, there is the option of technical and further education (or TAFE). Melbourne TAFE courses are typically more hands-on and are focused on providing students with the workplace skills and training needed by employers. TAFE facilities provide students with industry-standard equipment that allows them to train outside the classroom, such as automotive workshops and training restaurants that are open to the public. TAFE courses are designed with industry needs in mind, and many offer opportunities to complete on-the-job training through work experience.

TAFE institutes pride themselves on their accessibility and typically have fewer (and lower) entry requirements than universities.

There are also ample opportunities to study music, dance, theatre and visual arts at various levels. Afterall, Melbourne has long prided itself as Australia's arts capital. It has the theatres, galleries, bookshops, laneways, cafes and bars. The architecture, colonial and modern, is amazing. I believe that as a part of the educational process, each child should have access to a music or arts education program. That is part of a well-rounded education and can be a means of uncovering a child's hidden talent. This is something an education in Melbourne can offer.

Furthermore, there are education opportunities for children with learning difficulties and for gifted children. These are in schools with special programmes. There are also hospital schools, where children who need prolonged hospitalisation are educated, and special schools for blind and deaf children.

English is the official language of Australia and the language of instruction. Some schools offer bilingual programs or programs in other languages such as Mandarin, Vietnamese, Indonesian, and German. The school curriculum consistently takes an international perspective and schools have a strong multicultural spirit.

The academic year usually begins in February and runs through to December. Each year, the dates are slightly different so check your institution's website for the most current information.

TAFE, university and college websites usually publish calendars with important dates for enrolment, orientation programs, semester breaks, exams, and when exam results become available.

'Census' dates usually start before the academic year. These are the deadlines for making changes to your enrolment. For example, changes to your selected subjects, course withdrawal and payments may be due by the 'census' date. Ask your education institute about 'census' dates.

Chapter Four

Where to Live in Melbourne?

Your choice of where to live in Melbourne when you first arrive will strongly determine your initial impressions of your new life and reduce the level of culture shock you experience. The sights and sounds of a neighbourhood and suburb can either make you quite at home or feel uneasy.

Because Melbourne is a diverse and cosmopolitan city, where one chooses to live depends on individual circumstances. Are you migrating alone, as a couple, or with a family? If with a family, are the children very young or teenagers?

Different 'Burbs for Different Folks

Different suburbs in Melbourne can appeal to different types of people depending on their lifestyle, interests, and priorities. Here are a few examples:

Young professionals: If you are a young professional, you may be drawn to neighbourhoods such as Carlton, Fitzroy, Richmond, or South Yarra. These areas offer a vibrant atmosphere with plenty of cafes, bars, and entertainment options, as well as easy access to the city centre.

Families: If you have children, you may be interested in neighbourhoods such as Williamstown, Northcote, Box Hill, or Cranbourne. These areas offer good schools, family-friendly parks, and community activities, as well as a range of housing options.

Students: If you are a student, you may want to consider neighbourhoods such as Carlton, Footscray, or Brunswick. These areas offer easy access to universities, affordable housing options, and a lively social scene.

Nature lovers: If you enjoy outdoor recreation, you may be interested in suburbs such as St Kilda, Dandenong, or Frankston. These areas offer access to beaches, parks, and hiking trails, as well as a range of cultural and entertainment options.

Multicultural communities: If you are looking for a keen sense of cultural diversity, you may be interested in neighbourhoods such as Sunshine, Noble Park, or Dandenong. These areas offer a range of cultural festivals, markets, and dining options, as well as access to community services and support.

Art and culture lovers: If you are interested in art and culture, you may want to consider neighbourhoods such as Collingwood, Southbank, or Prahran. These areas offer access to galleries, museums, and theatres, as well as a thriving creative scene.

Sports fans: If you are a sports fan, you may be interested in suburbs such as Richmond, Docklands, or Footscray. These areas offer access to stadiums and sporting events, as well as a range of sports clubs and facilities.

Foodies: If you are a food lover, you may want to consider neighbourhoods such as Fitzroy, Brunswick, or South Yarra. These areas offer a diverse range of dining options, from street food to high-end restaurants, as well as markets and specialty food stores.

Retirees: If you are retired, you may want to consider suburbs such as Williamstown, Brighton, or Balwyn. These areas offer a relaxed and peaceful atmosphere, as well as access to parks, beaches, and community services.

Birds of the Same Feather Tend to Flock Together

It is natural for people to prefer to live in an area where there are familiar faces, familiar language and familiar culture. The saying "birds of the same feather flock together" seems to apply to where new migrants chose to live when they first came to Melbourne. They settled in pockets, preferring to stay close together, finding comfort in familiar faces. This clustering of migrants from particular countries is evident throughout Melbourne. Here are a few examples:

Chinese: Many Chinese migrants to Melbourne are drawn to suburbs such as Box Hill, Glen Waverley, or Doncaster, which have large

Chinese communities and offer easy access to Chinese grocery stores, restaurants, and cultural events (that is, Chinese cultural amenities).

Indian: Many Indian migrants to Melbourne are drawn to suburbs such as Cranbourne, Noble Park, or Point Cook, which offer a strong sense of cultural diversity and access to Indian cultural amenities.

Italian: Many Italian migrants to Melbourne are drawn to suburbs such as Carlton, Brunswick or Preston which offer a strong sense of Italian culture and heritage, as well as access to Italian cultural amenities.

Greek: Many Greek migrants to Melbourne are drawn to suburbs such as Oakleigh, Brunswick or Coburg which offer a strong sense of Greek culture and heritage, as well as access to Greek grocery stores, restaurants and cultural events.

Vietnamese: Many Vietnamese migrants to Melbourne are drawn to suburbs such as Footscray, Richmond or Springvale which offer a strong sense of Vietnamese culture and heritage, as well as access to Vietnamese cultural amenities.

Lebanese: Many Lebanese migrants to Melbourne are drawn to suburbs such as Coburg, Brunswick or Northcote which offer a strong sense of Lebanese culture and heritage as well as access to Lebanese cultural activities.

Sri Lankan: Many Sri Lankan migrants to Melbourne are drawn to suburbs such as Clayton, Glen Waverley or Mulgrave which offer a strong sense of Sri Lankan culture and heritage, as well as access to Sri Lankan grocery stores, restaurants and cultural events.

Turkish: Many Turkish migrants to Melbourne are drawn to suburbs such as Coburg, Brunswick or Preston which offer a strong sense of Turkish culture and heritage, as well as access to Turkish cultural amenities.

Korean: Many Korean migrants to Melbourne are drawn to suburbs such as Box Hill, Glen Waverley or Doncaster which offer a strong sense of Korean culture and heritage, as well as access to Korean cultural amenities.

Filipino: Many Filipino migrants to Melbourne are drawn to suburbs such as Footscray, Sunshine or Dandenong which offer a strong sense of Filipino culture and heritage, as well as access to Filipino cultural amenities.

Malaysian: Many Malaysian migrants to Melbourne are drawn to suburbs such as Clayton, Glen Waverley, or Box Hill, which offer a strong sense of Malaysian culture and heritage, as well as access to Malaysian grocery stores, restaurants, and cultural events.

Iranian: Many Iranian migrants to Melbourne are drawn to suburbs such as Brunswick, Coburg, or Preston, which offer a strong sense of Iranian culture and heritage, as well as access to Iranian grocery stores, restaurants, and cultural events.

Japanese: Many Japanese migrants to Melbourne are drawn to suburbs such as Richmond, South Yarra, or Brunswick, which offer a strong sense of Japanese culture and heritage, as well as access to Japanese cultural amenities.

Sudanese: Many Sudanese migrants to Melbourne are drawn to suburbs such as Sunshine, Dandenong, or Footscray, which offer a strong sense of Sudanese culture and heritage, as well as access to Sudanese cultural amenities.

Irish: Many Irish migrants to Melbourne are drawn to suburbs such as Brunswick, Fitzroy, or St Kilda, which offer a vibrant and lively social scene with plenty of pubs, bars, and live music venues.

Of course, not all migrants of a particular nationality will have the same preferences when it comes to choosing a suburb to live in Melbourne. The most suitable suburb for an individual, couple, or family will depend on their specific needs, priorities, and preferences. It is crucial to conduct extensive research, physically visit different areas, and engage with local residents to gain insight into which suburb may be the most suitable.

Most Expensive & Cheapest Suburbs in Melbourne

The cost of living in different suburbs of Melbourne can vary widely depending on factors such as location, housing type, and local amenities. Here are a few examples of some of the most expensive and cheapest suburbs in Melbourne:

Most Expensive Suburbs

These include:

Toorak - Known for its affluent residents and luxury homes, Toorak is consistently ranked as one of the most expensive suburbs in Melbourne with a reputation for luxury living.

South Yarra - Located close to the city centre and popular among young professionals, South Yarra has a high cost of living and is known for its expensive apartments and designer boutiques.

Brighton - A seaside suburb with a reputation for its high-end real estate, upscale shopping and dining options, and proximity to the beach. Brighton has some of Melbourne's most expensive real estate.

Hawthorn - Known for its leafy streets, historic homes, and upscale restaurants and cafes, Hawthorn is a sought-after suburb with a high cost of living.

Kew - Located just a few kilometres east of the CBD, Kew is known for its grand mansions, exclusive schools, and high-end shopping and dining options.

Armadale - Located about 7km southeast of the CBD, Armadale is known for its luxury homes, boutique shopping, and exclusive schools.

Balwyn - Located about 10km east of the CBD, Balwyn is a family-friendly suburb with a high cost of living and a range of high-end amenities, including restaurants, shops, and schools.

Cheapest suburbs

These include:

Melton - Located about 40km west of the CBD, Melton is a growing suburb known for its affordability and range of housing options, with a relatively low cost of living compared to some of Melbourne's more expensive suburbs.

Frankston - Located about 40km southeast of the CBD, this seaside suburb is known for its affordability, family-friendly atmosphere, and range of recreational activities.

Werribee - Located about 30km southwest of the CBD, Werribee is a growing suburb with a range of affordable housing options and a relatively low cost of living compared to some of Melbourne's more expensive suburbs.

Sunshine - Located about 12km west of the CBD, Sunshine is a diverse suburb with a range of affordable housing options and a relatively low cost of living.

Chapter Five

Money Matters

Many new migrants to Melbourne, having failed to plan their finances in detail beforehand, find that their savings are drying up much quicker than anticipated.

A social security system exists in Australia, providing people with a minimum adequate standard of living by a system of social welfare payments.

Your Financial Situation

While there are many things to consider when relocating to a new city, one of the most important aspects to think about is your finances. Money plays a critical role in ensuring a smooth transition to a new city, and it is important to plan and budget carefully to avoid financial stress and difficulties.

Here are some tips to help you manage your money when moving to Melbourne as a migrant:

Research the cost of living: Before moving to Melbourne, it is essential to research the cost of living in this city. This will help you plan and budget accordingly, so you can ensure you have enough money to cover your expenses. Consider the cost of housing, transportation, food, utilities and other necessary expenses.

Create a budget: Once you have an idea of the cost of living, create a budget to help you manage your money effectively. List your monthly income and expenses and allocate your funds accordingly. Be sure to factor in any additional costs associated with moving, such as transportation or storage fees.

Build an emergency fund: It is always a good idea to have some savings set aside for unexpected expenses, such as medical bills or car repairs. Consider setting up an emergency fund to cover unexpected costs and contribute to it regularly.

Explore job opportunities: Finding a job in a new city can be challenging, especially as a migrant. Research job opportunities in the area and consider networking with others in your field. If you are struggling to find work, consider taking on freelance or contract work to supplement your income.

Consider housing options: Housing can be one of the most significant expenses when moving to Melbourne. Consider different housing options, such as shared accommodation or renting a smaller apartment, to reduce your costs. Research the different neighbourhoods in the city to find an affordable and safe place to live.

Income Tax

In Melbourne, as in the rest of Australia, income tax rates depend on your circumstances. .

Here is the full tax table for residents for the 2022-23 financial year according to the Australian Taxation Office:

Please note that these rates do not include the Medicare levy of 2%
.

Double Taxation

Check whether you are liable for double taxation. Double taxation in Australia refers to a situation where an individual or company is taxed on the same income or asset in both Australia and another country. This can occur when you or your business has income or assets in Australia but is also taxed in your home country where you are a tax resident or where the income or assets are located.

To avoid double taxation, Australia has a foreign income tax offset (FITO) system that allows individuals to claim a credit for any foreign tax paid on the same income.

Cost of Living

An effective way of comparing the cost of living between the town or city where you live, and Melbourne, is to get feedback of prices for a "basket" of local stuff from local residents. To be sure of consistency, the idea is to compare apples with apples within the basket of stuff. So, if we have a pair of jeans in our basket, we must compare jeans of a similar brand.

There are various websites that provide cost of living comparisons amongst the cities of the world from the cost information provided by local residents. From these websites, the living cost in most cities can be compared with Melbourne.

The cost of living in Melbourne can be relatively high compared to other cities in Australia and other countries, especially when it comes to housing costs. However, there are ways to manage costs, such as living in more affordable suburbs, using public transportation, and taking advantage of free or low-cost activities and events.

Typical prices in Melbourne as of April 2023

Websites like numbeo.com and expatistan.com offer cost of living data for various cities, including Melbourne. Below is a table showing typical average prices for Melbourne, sourced from these and similar websites (as of 8th April 2023):

- Basic lunchtime menu (including a drink) in the CBD: AUD21

- Combo meal in fast food restaurant (Big Mac meal or similar): AUD14

- 1 litre (1 quart) of full cream milk: AUD1.77

- 12 eggs, large: AUD5.50

- Bread for 2 people for 1 day: AUD3.10

- Weekly rent for 2-bedroom, 1-bathroom apartment (1km

from CBD): AUD600-800

- Weekly rent for 2-bedroom, 1-bathroom apartment (5km from CBD): AUD500-680

- Regular petrol (standard unleaded) per litre: AUD1.90

- Monthly ticket public transport: AUD178

Welfare Net

If you are reading this in a country where you have to struggle on your own if you do not have a job to pay the food bills, home expenses, medical bills and other costs of living, then you will find Melbourne and Australia to be an unbelievable place to live in.

Social security in Australia refers to a system of social welfare payments provided by the Australian Government to eligible Australian citizens, permanent residents, and limited international visitors. These payments are almost always administered by Centrelink, a program of Services Australia. In Australia, most payments are means-tested. The primary purpose of Australia's transfer, or social security, system is to provide individuals with a 'minimum adequate standard of living.'

Families

Childcare subsidy – Assistance to help you with the cost of childcare.

Family Tax Benefit: A payment to help families with the cost of raising children, consisting of two components - Part A and Part B.

Newborn Upfront Payment and Newborn Supplement – a lump sum and an increase to your Family Tax Benefit Part A payment when you start caring for a baby or child that has recently come into your care.

Parenting Payment – The main income support payment while you are a young child's main carer for a child under 8 if you are single, or under 6 if you have a partner.

Youth and students

Austudy – Financial help if you are 25 or older and studying or an Australian Apprentice.

Youth Allowance – Financial help if you are 24 or younger and a student or Australian Apprentice.

Jobseekers

JobSeeker Payment – Financial help if you are between 22 and Age Pension age and looking for work. It is also for when you are sick or injured and cannot do your usual work or study for a short time.

Older Australians

Age Pension – A government payment for older Australians who meet age and residency requirements.

People with disability

Disability Support Pension – Financial help if you have a physical, intellectual or psychiatric condition that is likely to persist for more than 2 years and stops you from working.

Mobility Allowance – A payment to help with travel costs for work, study or looking for work if you have a disability, illness or injury that means you cannot use public transport.

Carers

Carer Payment – A payment if you give constant care to someone who has a severe disability, illness, or an adult who is frail aged.

Carer Allowance: A payment to assist those who provide care for a family member or friend with a disability or medical condition, but do not qualify for the Carer Payment.

Supplementary payments

Energy Supplement – A payment to help individuals on certain Centrelink payments with the cost of energy bills.

Pharmaceutical Allowance – A regular extra payment to help with medicine costs if you get certain Centrelink payments.

Rent Assistance – A regular extra payment if you pay rent and get certain Centrelink payments.

Waiting Period

New residents may have to wait *up to 4 years* before they can get some of these payments or concession cards.

Medical

You will probably also want to stay current with your health insurance (if you have one) until you are eligible for Medicare. Many people conveniently forget to tell their insurer that they are living in another country, which could cause complications and be very costly if a claim arises.

Your Home Options in Melbourne

Melbourne has a wide range of housing types, but you should be aware of a range of issues before buying. Renting makes lots of sense in a new city even if you can afford to buy.

Melbourne's range of housing types include:

Freestanding houses – also known as detached houses or standalone houses, are a type of residential building that are not attached to any other dwellings. They are separate structures that sit on their own block of land and are not connected to any other building, except for utility connections such as water, electricity, and gas.

Semi-detached houses – also known as duplexes or paired homes, are a type of residential building that are usually a mirror image of the adjoining neighbour's home. They share a common wall and often a common boundary fence.

Terrace houses – also known as row houses or linked houses, are a type of residential building that is attached to other terrace houses to form a row of identical or similar dwellings that share side walls. They can be single or double storey.

Villa units – also known as strata units or simply units, are a type of residential building amongst two or more similar units on a single block of land. They usually share a common wall with neighbours and almost always share common driveways and sometimes garden areas.

Townhouses – are a type of residential building that typically consist of several individual units on a single block of land, each with its own entrance and outdoor space. Townhouses are often two or three storeys tall and are designed to provide a balance of privacy and community living. Townhouses are similar to villa units and duplexes, but they are typically larger and may be part of a larger development, such as a townhouse complex or a gated community.

Apartments – are a type of residential building that are typically located within a larger building. Each apartment within the building is also referred to as a unit or apartment unit. Apartment buildings can be high-rise or tower blocks comprising hundreds of units and common amenities such as a lobby, gymnasium, swimming pool, resident lounge(s), meeting room(s), and rooftop garden. Alternatively, they can be smaller blocks, sometimes called boutique apartments, with 12, 20, or 36 units and minimal or no common amenities.

There are several other housing types that you may encounter in Melbourne, including studio units, granny flats, and penthouses. *Studio units* are a special kind of accommodation that typically combine a bedroom, living room, and kitchen into one room, and include an attached bathroom, commonly called an ensuite bathroom in Melbourne. A studio unit can be located among other units within a multi-unit complex or in an apartment building. A *granny flat* or in-law flat is a self-contained dwelling that is either within, attached to, or separate from the main family home on the same parcel of land. A *penthouse* is usually the largest apartment on the highest floor of an apartment building and can be either single-level or two-level.

Houses and apartments may be as little as a few months old, or anywhere up to 150 years old. They may be made of brick, concrete, or timber (sometimes called weatherboard). Many old dwellings in Melbourne have been completely refurbished, particularly internally, featuring modern surfaces, appliances, fixtures and fittings. Dwellings usually include one to four bedrooms, a living room, dining area, kitchen, one or two bathrooms, a laundry room, and a car garage or carport. Larger homes also include a second or third living room (such as a family room, games room, home cinema or rumpus room), a third bathroom, and a powder room. Melburnians in general love the sun, hence many homes feature an outdoor entertaining area.

Most homes have heating, and some have central cooling or separate air-conditioning units. Carpets, curtains or blinds, light fittings, kitchen cupboards, hot water systems and stoves/ovens are generally included. Most homes include built-in wardrobes and some a dishwasher.

Fully furnished houses are not common in Victoria. So, you may need to purchase items such as refrigerators, washing machines, clothes dryers, beds, tables, chairs and sofas or lounge suites.

Buying Your Home

After arriving in Melbourne, when you have decided on which suburb or where within a suburb to live in, the type of home that suits your needs and the price range that you can afford, then you should be aware of a range of issues before buying. A list of these issues is presented below:

- In Victoria, by law, you are to receive a *Vendor's Statement* (also known as a Section 32 Statement) signed by the vendor in accordance with Section 32 of the Sale of Land Act, with a copy attached to the contract. The statement contains prescribed information which, if incorrect or insufficient, may enable you to avoid the contract or sue the vendor for damages. This statement should contain information relating to the Title, Easements and Covenants, Rates and Charges, Notices and Orders, Services, Planning and Building Permits. But there are some matters not disclosed in the Vendor's Statement such as whether any buildings breach any provisions of the Victorian Building Regulations; or whether there are any defects or problems with any buildings and fittings on the property (e.g., leaky roof, infestation of white ants, heating equipment not functioning etc.)

- Check the *title and plans*. Who is the owner? There were cases whereby an innocent buyer purchased a home from a fraudulent seller who was not the legal owner of the property! Is the property subject to a mortgage? Are there any caveats, easements or covenants shown on title and what do they mean? For example, an easement can be a burden to a property. Make sure the actual boundaries on the land match those on the plans. If you are not sure, engage a professional land surveyor.

- Be aware of all *costs of buying* a home, which include legal and conveyancing fees; loan establishment fees; building and pest inspection fees; a pre-purchase valuation (for peace of mind); government charges such as *land transfer duty* (formerly known as stamp duty), GST and fire services levy. You should investigate whether you will be required to pay a growth area infrastructure contribution.

- Also, be aware of *on-going costs* of owning a home including building insurance, Council rates and land tax (if applicable).

- As a home buyer, it is important to establish from the agent or the Vendor that *vacant possession* will be given at settlement, and the Contract will need to clearly stipulate "vacant possession."

- If the property is tenanted, check the *terms of the Lease*. How long has the lease to run? Who pays the outgoings? What's the tenant's history?

- If the property is a unit within an apartment building, villa unit development or any multi-unit complex with common property such as driveways or grounds, it may be subject to an *owner's corporation*. You may be required to pay fees and follow rules that restrict what you can do on your property, such as a ban on pet ownership.

- While the above unit you are considering will usually be strata titled, some may be *company titled or stratum titled*. These other types of title will affect your ownership, rights and responsibilities in different ways.

- A *cooling-off period* of three clear business days applies to private sales of residential property sales regardless of price. The cooling-off period gives you time to consider the offer. It begins from the date you sign the contract, not from the date the seller signs it. To cool off, you must give written notice to the seller or the seller's agent. You will be entitled to a full refund of money paid, less $100 or 0.2 per cent of the purchase price, whichever is greater. However, there are situations where the cooling-off period does not apply. These include when the property was purchased at a public auction, or you previously signed a contract for the same property with the same terms.

- If you find *problems with the building work* in your new home, repair work may be covered by warranties and insurance.

- If *two or more people* are buying the property together, you need to specify whether ownership is joint or as tenants-in-common in the land transfer document. There are some other alternatives which will involve drawing up a Declaration of Trust.

- The buyer is responsible for paying *land transfer duty*. This duty is calculated as a percentage of the purchase price or the market value of the property, whichever is greater. Duty applies to the GST-inclusive price of a new property. It is usually paid at settlement, but the buyer has up to three months after settlement to pay. The buyer cannot receive title to a property until they have paid the duty.

- Do not overlook *any concessions* you may be eligible for, such as: first homeowners grant for buyers of new homes and land transfer duty reduction.

Renting Might be a Better Option

Renting makes lots of sense in a new city even if you can afford to buy. Renting allows you to test the waters in a new city before committing to purchasing a property. You can get a feel for the neighbourhood and area's amenities and decide whether you want to stay in the area long-term.

Renting allows you to live in a desirable location that may be unaffordable if you were to purchase a property. You can choose to rent in a location that is close to work, school, or other amenities that are important to you.

How much rent you can afford to pay will be a key factor in selecting where you live and what type of home you live in. In Melbourne, rentals are usually quoted as a weekly rent. Multiply the weekly rent by 52 weeks in a year to get the amount of rent you will pay for an entire year. Divide the year's rent by 12 to get the monthly rent, which is the rental payment you will pay to the landlord in advance for the coming month.

Compare rents in different suburbs and precincts within suburbs to get a good idea of what you are getting for your money. There could be big differences in rentals for a similar type of property in neighbouring suburbs or different types of properties in one suburb.

How to Find a Property to Buy or Rent?

Properties are generally purchased or rented through real estate agents, but you can also buy or rent directly from the owner. Many real estate agents produce a weekly sales and rental list of available properties. There are also websites and city-wide and local newspapers available to help you find a home to buy or rent.

An option that is becoming common in Melbourne is to use the services of a buyer's agent or buyer's advocate. This licensed professional will assist you every step of the way, including searching a home meeting your specifications, getting a market valuation, negotiating or bidding at auctions and ensuring all documentation is in order.

Chapter Six

Medical Care in Melbourne

Melbourne has a high-quality healthcare system that is accessible to all residents.

Melbourne also has several nurse advice and triage services that you can access for non-emergency medical advice and support.

If you are experiencing a medical emergency, you should call triple zero (000) or go to your nearest hospital emergency department.

Melbourne has a high-quality healthcare system that is accessible to all residents. Here are some key things to know about medical care in Melbourne:

Public Healthcare: Australia has a public healthcare system known as Medicare, which provides free or subsidised medical treatment for Australian citizens and permanent residents. This includes access to public hospitals, general practitioners, and specialists. If you are a new migrant and eligible for Medicare, you will need to register with Medicare by visiting a Medicare service centre.

Private Healthcare: Melbourne also has a range of private healthcare providers, including private hospitals, clinics, and specialists. Private healthcare can be more expensive than public healthcare, but it may offer shorter wait times and more personalised care.

Health Insurance: While Medicare provides basic healthcare coverage, many Australians choose to supplement this with private health insurance. Private health insurance can provide additional benefits, such as coverage for dental and optical services, and may also provide access to private hospitals and specialists. If you are considering private health insurance, it is important to research different providers and policies to find one that suits your needs and budget.

Pharmacies: Melbourne has many pharmacies (known as "chemists" in Australia) where you can purchase prescription and over-the-counter medications. Some pharmacies also offer additional services, such as flu vaccinations and health checks.

Emergency Care: In case of a medical emergency, you can call triple zero (000) for an ambulance. But, note that in Victoria, unless you have an Ambulance Victoria membership, concession entitlement or other coverage, you can expect to pay $1,306 for an ambulance trip in the city and $1,927 if you're in a regional or rural area to cover the cost (effecive 3 July 2023). Melbourne has several public hospitals with emergency departments that provide emergency care 24/7.

In addition to the abovementioned healthcare services, Melbourne also has several nurse advice and triage services that you can access for non-emergency medical advice and support. Here are a few examples:

Nurse on Call: This 24/7 phone service provides free advice and information from a registered nurse for residents of Victoria. You can call 1300 60 60 24 to speak to a nurse about your health concerns and get advice on what to do next.

Health Direct: This national telehealth service provides 24/7 phone and online advice from a registered nurse. You can call 1800 022 222 or visit the Health Direct website to speak to a nurse about your health concerns and get advice on what to do next.

After Hours GP Helpline: This 24/7 phone service provides free advice and information from a GP for residents of Victoria. You can call 1800 022 222 to speak to a GP about your health concerns and get advice on what to do next.

Mental Health Services: Melbourne has several mental health services that you can access for support and advice if you are experiencing mental health issues. These include services such as Lifeline (13 11 14), Beyond Blue (1300 22 4636), and Headspace (1800 650 890).

These services can be a helpful resource if you are not sure what to do about a health concern or need advice on whether to seek medical attention. However, it is important to remember that these services are not a substitute for medical care, and if you are experiencing a medical emergency, you should call triple zero (000) or go to your nearest hospital emergency department.

Chapter Seven

Overcoming the Fear of Moving to a New City

F ear of change is one of the most common reasons for resisting change because it stops you taking any action at all. But it is not the only fear.

Moving to a New City is Stressful

Depending on which survey you look at, moving home is among the top 5 most stressful things that people may experience. Damaged and misplaced possessions and finding out that furniture does not fit in the new home topped the list of most stressful moving day moments. Some survey results also showed that moving home beats starting a new job, divorce and relationship breakdown, all joint second in the stress stakes.

So, moving to a new city in a different country can understandably cause significant anxiety. The thought of relocating from your hometown to a distant place like Melbourne, can trigger a myriad of concerns, even for the most adventurous individuals. These concerns often revolve around the fear of change, the unknown, loss, failure, and self-doubt. Questions of where, which, what if, how, when, etc. are likely to lead to many sleepless nights. These questions could include:

1. What is the cost of living in the new city? Will it be affordable to live there comfortably?

2. How will the move impact your job or career? Will you be able to find employment in your field?

3. How will the move impact your social support system? Will you have friends or family nearby?

4. How will you adjust to a new climate or weather patterns in the new city?

5. How will the move impact your mental and emotional well-being?

6. Will you be able to maintain a healthy work-life balance in the new city?

7. Will you be able to find suitable housing and neighbourhoods that meet your needs?

8. Will you be able to adapt to a new culture or way of life in the new city?

9. What are the transportation options in the new city, and how will you get around?

10. How will the move impact your children or family members, if any, who are coming with you?

11. Where should I live in Melbourne? Which suburb?

12. Which school should I enrol my son / daughter in?

13. What if my migration application is rejected?

14. What if my spouse does not like Melbourne?

15. When should I make my move? As soon as my application is approved. Or when?

Fear of Change

Fear of change is one of the most common reasons for resisting change because it stops you taking any action at all. And if nothing changes, nothing will change in your current situation. If you continue to do the same thing, continue your routine, continue your life as it is, then do not expect any change to occur. Because if you do (expect change but continue doing the same thing), then that is the definition of lunacy!

In most cases, fear of change stops us from taking action. We are often frozen with fear and prefer to remain in our comfort zone instead of taking action to change or improve our situation. Fear of change often works with anxiety, self-doubt and guilt to help it to do this.

Some anxiety or stress can be a good thing because it gets us to do something. But there are times when feeling anxious about something new can really limit us. This often happens if we are uncertain about the future. High levels of anxiety are often a result of self-doubt and not knowing what to expect. Feeling anxious can stop us trying something new and makes us resist change by stirring up fears of what is not known. Feeling guilty about leaving family members or even friends behind can also cause us to fear change.

Several other common fears to change can also prevent you from making the move to Melbourne. These extend to:

Fear of the Unknown

Like it or not we are creatures of habit. We like our routines and do not like to be faced with the unknown. Not knowing what to expect when we arrive in Melbourne could be a contributing cause of our anxiety. This fear seems more stressful when we do not have enough information about Melbourne, and we are expected to take a 'leap of faith'. This can result in a lot of anxious feelings.

Fear of Failure

The fear that could be caused by "failed" migration stories about those who left for another country expecting a better life only to return after several years due to a variety of reasons. The fear of failure makes us want to avoid the pain of failing by not doing anything at all. "Don't talk to me about starting a new life in Melbourne!"

Fear of Loss

By moving to Melbourne to start a new life you may be giving up a cushy job, a profitable business or a comfortable life. Change can mean loss of good friends, loss of a stable income, or even loss of your favourite local food joints. Other losses could include the loss of your weekly game routine, your job title, or the nice park across the street.

Self-Doubt

"I won't get enough points in my migration application.," "My qualifications will not be recognised...," I can't compete with the local businesses in Melbourne...." These are examples of doubting yourself. Not only do you start believing this about yourself, but you fear that others might see this too. The easy way out is to resist change. Forget about giving yourself a second chance in Melbourne and you put that aspiration away. Putting yourself down in this way is a result of a lack of confidence and a fear of change that stops one taking any action. It literally stops us getting ahead in life.

Overcoming Your Different Fears

From my own life experiences, I find that the best ways to overcoming my fears and self-doubt are as follows:

1. *Have a reason, goal or why that is much stronger than your fears.* If you deeply and truly have a strong desire to want to give yourself a

second chance and a new life in Melbourne, your mind will somehow diminish your fears. The thoughts of a happier, healthier and wealthier life will overshadow your fears, just like how the fragrance of an air freshener counteracts a bad smell!

2. *Find out as much as possible about life in Melbourne.* Reading this book from cover to cover is a good start. Ignorance causes unnecessary worry. When you have enough information and knowledge about an area that is causing you fear, that fear can be eliminated. Use the areas that are raised in this book as your starting point. So, if one of your fears is about not being able to find a job in Melbourne, go online and fire up Google. Enter keyword searches such as "Melbourne job opportunities," "Melbourne jobs," "working in Melbourne," "finding work in Melbourne," etc. If another fear is about a suitable school for your children, then Google "Melbourne schools," "Melbourne good school guide," etc. You got the idea.

3. *Take action.* For example, if you worry about not meeting the migration requirements to Australia, do something about the areas that you lack. If it is your incompetency in English, take an English course. If it is a lack of a qualification, work towards getting it.

Chapter Eight

What's Next?

A ustralia is a multicultural society that has a long history of welcoming migrants from all over the world. Yes, migrants are wanted, needed, and welcomed in Melbourne.

Are You Wanted?

Yes, migrants are wanted, needed, and welcome in Melbourne. Australia is a multicultural society that has a long history of welcoming migrants from all over the world, and Melbourne is one of the most diverse and inclusive cities in the world.

Migrants have made significant contributions to the social, cultural, and economic life of Melbourne, and are an integral part of the city's identity. Melbourne is home to a large and vibrant migrant community, with residents from a wide range of backgrounds and cultures.

The Australian government and various organisations in Melbourne actively encourage skilled migrants to migrate to the city and contribute to its economy and social fabric. There are many programs and initiatives in place to help migrants settle in Melbourne and find employment, education, and other essential services.

Overall, Melbourne is a welcoming and inclusive city that values diversity and encourages the participation of migrants in all aspects of society.

On 2 September 2022, the Australian Government announced that the planning level for the 2022-23 permanent Migration Program will increase to 195,000 places. The Government announced a detailed composition of the Migration Program as part of the Budget delivered on 25 October 2022.

The 2022-23 Migration Program will help ease critical workforce shortages where the skilling of Australians cannot yet keep pace with industry demand. The Migration Program will have a planning level of 195,000 visa places. The Program has the following composition:

Skill (142,400 places) – this stream is designed to improve the productive capacity of the economy and fill skill shortages in the labour market, including those in regional Australia.

Family (52,500 places) – this stream is predominantly made up of Partner visas, enabling Australians to reunite with family members from overseas and provide them with pathways to citizenship.

From 2022-23, Partner visas will be granted on a demand driven basis to facilitate family reunification. This will help reduce the Partner visa pipeline and processing times for many applicants.

40,500 *Partner* visas are estimated for 2022-23 for planning purposes, noting this estimate is not subject to a ceiling.

3,000 *Child visas* are estimated for 2022-23 for planning purposes, noting this category is demand driven and not subject to a ceiling.

Special Eligibility (100 places) – this stream covers visas for those in special circumstances, including permanent residents returning to Australia after a period overseas.

But to be accepted for migration to Australia you must meet the personal and occupational requirements of the category for which you are applying and be of good health and character.

Categories for Migration

There are several categories of migration to Australia:

Skilled migration: This category is for individuals who have skills and qualifications that are in demand in Australia. Skilled migration is a points-based system, and applicants must meet certain criteria, such as age, language proficiency, work experience, and education.

Family migration: This category is for individuals who have family members in Australia, such as spouses, parents, children, and other relatives. Family members who are Australian citizens, permanent residents, or eligible New Zealand citizens can sponsor their family members for migration to Australia.

Humanitarian migration: This category is for individuals who are fleeing persecution, war, or other humanitarian crises in their home countries. Australia offers protection to refugees and other displaced persons through its humanitarian migration program.

Business and investment migration: This category is for individuals who have a significant amount of money to invest in Australia or who want to start a business in Australia. Applicants must meet certain criteria, such as having a successful business background or a high net worth.

Student migration: This category is for individuals who want to study in Australia. Students can apply for a student visa, which allows them to stay in Australia for the duration of their studies. After completing their studies, students may be eligible for other types of visas, such as skilled migration visas.

Working holiday visa: This category is for individuals aged 18-30 (35 for some countries) who want to holiday in Australia and work to fund their trip. The visa is valid for up to 12 months and allows the holder to work for up to six months with each employer.

Temporary skilled visa: This category is for individuals who are sponsored by an employer to work in a specific skilled occupation in Australia on a temporary basis. The visa is valid for up to four years and may be extended in some circumstances.

Distinguished talent visa: This category is for individuals who are recognised internationally for exceptional talent in a specific field. This visa allows the holder to live and work in Australia permanently.

Each of these categories has specific eligibility criteria and application processes, and it is important to consult with a migration agent or the Department of Home Affairs to determine which category is best suited to your circumstances.

It is beyond the scope of this book to go into the details of each of the above categories. But one key factor is the age limit for the certain categories. Therefore, if you want a new life in Melbourne, begin making plans and act towards this goal before it is too late. Remember, the Australian migration application process could take several years.

IMPORTANT NOTE: Australian migration policy, including quotas, categories, and eligibility criteria, changes periodically. For the most up-to-date information, please visit the official website: https://immi.homeaffairs.gov.au

Option 2

If you are not ready or cannot migrate to Melbourne to start a new life for whatever reason, a second option could be:

- finding a product from where you live to export to Melbourne.

- importing something from a Melbourne supplier to distribute to your country.

- providing virtual services to Melbourne companies such as administrative and secretarial support.

- organising tours to Melbourne for your country men and women.

- organising in-bound tours to tourist spots in your country for Melburnians.

- representing a Melbourne college and promoting their courses in your country.

APPENDICES

Appendix A

Australia Quick Facts

Australia, officially known as the Commonwealth of Australia, is a country comprising:

- the mainland of the Australian continent;

- the island of Tasmania; and

- numerous smaller islands.

It has an area of 7.692 million square kilometres (or 2.979 million square miles), making it the world's sixth-largest country by total area.

Neighbouring countries include Papua New Guinea, Indonesia and East Timor to the north; the Solomon Islands and Vanuatu to the north-east; and New Zealand to the south-east.

According to the Australian Bureau of Statistics, Australia's population was 26,124,814 people on 30 September 2022.

Australia is an advanced country and one of the wealthiest in the world, with the world's thirteenth largest economy as of 2021. In 2020, Australia had the ninth highest per capita income in the world, according to the International Monetary Fund. With the third-highest human development index globally, Australia ranks highly in many international comparisons of national performance, such as quality of life, health, education, economic freedom, and the protection of civil liberties and political rights.

Appendix B

Melbourne Quick Facts

- Melbourne is the capital, largest and most populous city in Victoria, and the second most populous city in Australia and Oceania. It is also the business, administrative, cultural and recreational hub of the state.

- The name "Melbourne" refers to the area of urban agglomeration (as well as a census statistical division) spanning 9,900 square kilometres (or 3,800 square miles) which comprises the broader metropolitan area, as well as being the common name for its city centre.

- Melbourne is located around the large natural bay of Port Phillip, which is a large natural harbour that stretches over 1,930 square kilometres (745 square miles). The urban area of Melbourne extends from the city centre, which is located on the northern shore of the bay, outwards in all directions. To the east, the city extends into the Dandenong Ranges, which are a series of low mountain ranges that are located about 35 kilometres (22 miles) from the city centre.

- To the north, the city extends to the outer suburbs and regional areas such as Craigieburn and Sunbury. To the west, Melbourne extends to the Werribee River, which is located approximately 25 kilometres (16 miles) from the city centre, and includes suburbs such as Footscray, Sunshine, and Werribee.

- To the south, the city extends to the Mornington Peninsula, which is a large area of land that is located on the southern shore of Port Phillip Bay. The peninsula is home to many popular tourist attractions, such as the seaside towns of Portsea and Sorrento, and is also known for its wineries and natural beauty.

- Melbourne (or Greater Melbourne) is divided into 31 municipalities (or Local Government Areas), each with its own local government council. These LGAs are responsible for providing a range of services to residents, including local roads, waste collection, planning and zoning, and community services.

- Each municipality has its own unique character and attractions, and together they form the vibrant and diverse metropolitan area of Melbourne.

- The greater Melbourne metropolitan area has a total of around 312 suburbs, spread across the 31 LGAs. The number of suburbs in each LGA varies, with some having more than others. Here is a breakdown of the LGAs and number of suburbs in each LGA:

City of Melbourne - 14 suburbs
City of Banyule - 13 suburbs
City of Bayside - 8 suburbs
City of Boroondara - 11 suburbs
City of Brimbank - 19 suburbs
City of Cardinia - 20 suburbs
City of Casey - 21 suburbs
City of Darebin - 13 suburbs
City of Frankston - 10 suburbs
City of Glen Eira - 9 suburbs
City of Greater Dandenong - 10 suburbs

City of Hobsons Bay - 7 suburbs

City of Hume - 18 suburbs

City of Kingston - 12 suburbs

City of Knox - 16 suburbs

City of Manningham - 13 suburbs

City of Maribyrnong - 10 suburbs

City of Maroondah - 13 suburbs

City of Melbourne - 14 suburbs

City of Melton - 18 suburbs

City of Monash - 14 suburbs

City of Moonee Valley - 10 suburbs

City of Moreland - 16 suburbs

City of Mornington Peninsula - 17 suburbs

City of Nillumbik - 11 suburbs

City of Port Phillip - 9 suburbs

City of Stonnington - 9 suburbs

City of Whitehorse - 12 suburbs

City of Whittlesea - 26 suburbs

City of Wyndham - 27 suburbs

City of Yarra - 7 suburbs

Note:

Boundaries of suburbs and LGAs are subject to change, and these numbers may fluctuate over time as new suburbs are created or merged.

- Melbourne residents enjoy a temperate climate influenced by its location at the apex of one of the world's largest bays, Port Phillip Bay.

- The official language is English, but more than 100 languages are spoken by the city's residents.

Appendix C

Government

The state of Victoria, of which Melbourne is the capital, is governed according to the principles of the Westminster system, a form of parliamentary government based on the model of the United Kingdom. Legislative power rests with the Parliament of Victoria, which consists of the Crown, represented by the Governor of Victoria, and the two Houses: the Upper House (Victorian Legislative Council) and the Lower House (Victorian Legislative Assembly).

Executive power rests formally with the Executive Council, which consists of the Governor and senior ministers. In practice, executive power is exercised by the Premier of Victoria and the Cabinet, who are appointed by the Governor, but who hold office by virtue of their ability to command the support of a majority of members of the Legislative Assembly.

Judicial power is exercised by the Supreme Court of Victoria and a system of subordinate courts, but the High Court of Australia and other federal courts have overriding jurisdiction on matters which fall under the ambit of the Australian Constitution.

Public administration in Victoria

Victoria's public service has a reputation as one of the best in Australia. Areas in which Victoria is particularly strong include road safety; water efficiency; the liveability of Melbourne; efforts to address family violence; and the efficiency and effectiveness of its service delivery.

Elections

Melburnians aged 18 years and over, vote to elect representatives to local councils and state and federal parliaments to make decisions on their behalf. Australia is a representative democracy in which voting is a fundamental right. We elect representatives at each of the three levels of government; local council, State and Federal to make decisions on our behalf at regular intervals.

This means Melburnians have someone to represent them at each level of government. Free and fair elections are central to our democracy. It is every citizen's responsibility to understand the electoral process and have a say.

At each election you get to decide how you would like to be represented in government, by choosing which party or candidate best represents your views.

Local council elections are held on the fourth Saturday of October every four years. Local councils make decisions about services in your neighbourhood.

State elections are held on the last Saturday of November every four years.

Victoria is divided into 88 districts (the Lower House) and eight regions (the Upper House). In a State election, you vote for one representative for your district and five representatives for your region.

If a district vacancy occurs during the term of the Parliament, a by-election is conducted.

If you come from a country where elections are marred with politicians insulting one another, vote rigging, money politics and one-sided news coverage, you will surely be impressed with the generally orderly way elections are held in Australia, whether in local, state or federal elections.

Who administers elections?

The Victorian Electoral Commission (VEC) is responsible for administering Victorian State elections. The VEC also administers Victorian council elections. Again, if you live in a country where elections are not fairly conducted, you will appreciate the impartiality of the VEC.

Appendix D

Resources for New Migrants to Melbourne

There are many resources available for new migrants to Melbourne to help them settle into their new home and community. Some of these resources include:

- *Settlement services:* The Australian government provides a range of settlement services for new migrants, including orientation sessions, language classes, and assistance with finding housing and employment. Visit https://immi.homeaffairs.gov.au/settling-in-australia/amep/overview

- *Community organisations:* There are many community organisations in Melbourne that provide support and resources for migrants, including advocacy, social services, and cultural events.

- *Libraries:* Melbourne has a great network of public libraries that offer free access to books, newspapers, and other resources, as well as language learning materials and community programs.

- *Employment services:* There are many employment services in Melbourne that specialise in helping new migrants find work, including resume writing, job search assistance, and language support.

- *Health services:* Melbourne has a comprehensive healthcare system, and new migrants can access a range of health services, including general practitioners, specialists, and hospitals. Visit www.health.vic.gov.au/primary-care/nurse-on-call

- *Legal services:* There are many legal services available in Melbourne that can assist new migrants with issues such as immigration, employment law, and human rights. Visit www.legalaid.vic.gov.au

- *Community centres:* Melbourne has many community centres that provide a range of services and resources for new migrants, including language classes, social events, and legal advice.

- *Housing support:* Finding suitable housing can be a challenge for new migrants, particularly those who are unfamiliar with the local rental market. There are many organisations in Melbourne that offer housing support services, including assistance with finding accommodation, understanding rental agreements, and accessing rental subsidies.

- *Home buying:* Visit www.your-new-home.com.au

- *Online resources:* There are many online resources available for new migrants, including government websites, community forums, and social media groups.

- *Childcare services:* For new migrant families with young children, accessing affordable and high-quality childcare can be a key concern. There are many childcare services available in Melbourne, including long day care, family day care, and after-school care programs.

- *Transport services:* Melbourne has an extensive public transport network, including buses, trains, and trams. New migrants may find it useful to familiarise themselves with the transport system and understand how to access concession fares and other discounts. Visit www.ptv.vic.gov.au/timetables

- *Cultural services:* Melbourne is a culturally diverse city, with many cultural events and festivals throughout the year. New migrants may find it helpful to connect with cultural organisations and attend cultural events to learn more about their new community and meet new people.

- *Financial services:* Managing finances can be challenging for new migrants, particularly those who are unfamiliar with the Australian banking and taxation system. There are many financial services available in Melbourne that can assist with banking, budgeting, and taxation advice.

- *Sports and recreation:* Participating in sports and recreational activities can be a wonderful way for new migrants to stay active and healthy, as well as meet new people. Melbourne has many sports and recreation facilities, including community centres, gyms, and parks.

- *Religious organisations:* Melbourne is home to many religious organisations, and new migrants may find it helpful to connect with a local religious community for support and fellowship.

- *Volunteer opportunities:* Volunteering is a wonderful way for new migrants to get involved in their new community, meet new people, and gain valuable experience. There are many volunteer organisations in Melbourne that offer a range of opportunities, including community service, environmental projects, and cultural events.

- *Home valuation services:* This could save you lots of money. Visit www.askthevaluer.com.au

- *English language classes:* Many organisations in Melbourne offer English language classes for migrants, including community centres, libraries, and language schools. These classes can help new migrants improve their language skills and communicate more effectively in their new community.

Printed in Dunstable, United Kingdom